The Scarlet Letter

NATHANIEL HAWTHORNE

Level 2

Retold by Chris Rice
Series Editors: Andy Hopkins and Jocelyn Potter

Pearson Education Limited
Edinburgh Gate, Harlow,
Essex CM20 2JE, England
and Associated Companies throughout the world.

ISBN: 978-1-4058-5534-1

First published in the USA by Ticknor, Reed, and Fields 1850
Published in the Penguin English Library 1970
First published by Penguin Books 2000
This edition published 2008

5 7 9 10 8 6

Typeset by Graphicraft Ltd, Hong Kong
Set in 11/14pt Bembo
Printed in China
SWTC/05

Published by Pearson Education Ltd in association with
Penguin Books Ltd, a Penguin Random House company.

For a complete list of the titles available in the Penguin Readers series please write to your local
Pearson Longman office or to: Penguin Readers Marketing Department, Pearson Education,
Edinburgh Gate, Harlow, Essex CM20 2JE, England.

Contents

Introduction

"I only want to know one thing," Chillingworth said. "Who is the father of this child?"

Hester looked him in the eye and said, "Do not ask. You will never know."

"Maybe the town will never know your secret," the old doctor said. "But I will find this man. I will know him when I see him. And then he will be mine!"

Boston, Massachusetts, is only twenty years old. It is a small town with one square, one church—and a small prison. One morning in June, the prison door opens and a beautiful woman comes out. Her name is Hester Prynne. There is a baby in her arms and a scarlet letter "A" on her dress—"A" for *adulteress*. Who is the father of her baby? Nobody knows, and Hester will not say. Then a strange, old man comes into town, and Hester feels very afraid. Who is this man? What is he going to do, and why is Hester Prynne afraid of him?

Nathaniel Hawthorne (1804–64) was born in Salem, Massachusetts. After college, he lived in Salem and started to write. People did not like his stories for a long time. Then he wrote his short stories, *Twice-Told Tales* (1837), and Hawthorne was famous. But he was not rich. He had to do other work for money. He worked in an office and on a farm. In 1842 he married and lived in Concord, Massachusetts. He lost his office job in 1849, and suddenly had more time for writing. He wrote *The Scarlet Letter* in 1850. People think that this is Hawthorne's greatest book. Hester Prynne is one of the most famous women in early American writing.

Chapter 1   Hester Prynne

In the 1600s, Boston, Massachusetts, was only a small town. Outside the town there was a small, dark building. This was the prison.

One morning in June a large crowd of people waited outside the prison door. They wore dark clothes.

"Hester Prynne is a child of the Devil," said an ugly woman in the crowd.

"That is right," said a man in a tall, gray hat. "Why don't they punish her with fire?"

"Why don't they kill her?" a third person wanted to know.

"Be quiet!" somebody called from the front of the crowd. "They are opening the prison door."

The crowd was quiet. The door opened and a small man in black clothes came out. A woman in a colorful dress followed him. She was a tall woman with a strong, beautiful face and large, dark eyes. Her long, black hair shone in the sunlight. There was a baby in her arms and a big, red letter "A" on the front of her dress.

"Look at her!" one woman in the crowd said angrily. "Those are not the clothes of an adulteress!"

"This is not punishment," the man in the tall, gray hat said. "The Governor is too kind."

"The woman will have her punishment!" the small man in black clothes said loudly to the crowd. "She will stand in the town square for four hours. Everybody will look at her and see her sin." He then turned to the woman with the baby and said, "Come, Hester Prynne, show your scarlet letter in the town square. Follow me."

Hester Prynne followed the small man through the crowd,

down the road to the town center. She walked slowly and held her head high. In the town square, in front of Boston's earliest church, she stood on a high platform with the baby in her arms.

The townspeople followed her into the square. They wanted to see this sinful woman with a baby but no husband. Some people looked at her quietly. Other people shouted at her angrily. Hester held the baby to her breast and thought about her home in Old England.

She remembered her mother and father, and then she remembered another man—a thin man with a tired, old face. This man was her husband. First he took her to Europe, to Amsterdam. Then he wanted to start a new life in New England. He sent Hester before him.

She arrived in the small town of Boston and waited for him. But he never came. Now, two years later, she stood on a platform in the middle of town with a scarlet letter on her breast and with a baby in her arms. A thousand eyes watched her, full of hate.

Suddenly, somebody spoke above the noise of the crowd: "Listen to me, Hester Prynne." Hester looked up. There was a large house near the platform. John Wilson, the oldest church minister in Boston, stood at an upstairs window. He looked down at her with cold, gray eyes and said, "Hester Prynne. Your minister wants to talk to you. Listen to him, please."

The people in the square and Hester looked up at the young man next to Wilson. It was Arthur Dimmesdale, one of the youngest ministers in the town. He looked at Hester for a minute with sad eyes and then started to speak.

"Hester Prynne," he said. "You have to tell us the name of the child's father. It will help you in the eyes of God. Tell us, please."

"I will not," Hester said.

"Woman!" John Wilson said loudly. "Listen to the good young man. Tell us the name of the father. Say that you are sorry. Then maybe we will take the scarlet letter from your breast."

"Hester Prynne," he said. "You have to tell us the name of the child's father."

"Never!" Hester answered loudly. She turned to the young minister again and looked into his eyes. "The scarlet letter is not only on my breast," she said. "It is inside my heart. You cannot take it from me."

"Speak!" somebody in the crowd shouted. "Give your child a father!"

"I will not speak," said Hester. "My child has a Father in Heaven. She will never have a father in this world."

Hester stood for four long hours on the platform in the town square. The old minister shouted at her, but she did not listen. She watched the crowd. She could not take her eyes off the angry faces. Then, at the back, she saw an old man. He had a tired, intelligent face. He looked at her with a strange smile.

"No, this is not possible," she thought.

The baby in her arms started to cry.

Chapter 2   Roger Chillingworth

At one o'clock they took Hester and her child back to the prison. Hester sat on the bed with her baby and cried. After an hour, she and the baby started to feel weak. The workers in the prison brought in a doctor. His name was Roger Chillingworth. Hester looked at the doctor and felt afraid. He was the man from the back of the crowd.

"Leave me with the young woman," the old doctor told the prison-workers.

He gave the baby something on a spoon. Minutes later, the baby stopped crying and slept. The doctor then turned to Hester Prynne and said, "Drink this. You will feel better."

Hester took a cup from his hand and drank slowly. Then she sat on the bed next to her baby. The doctor sat on the only chair in the room.

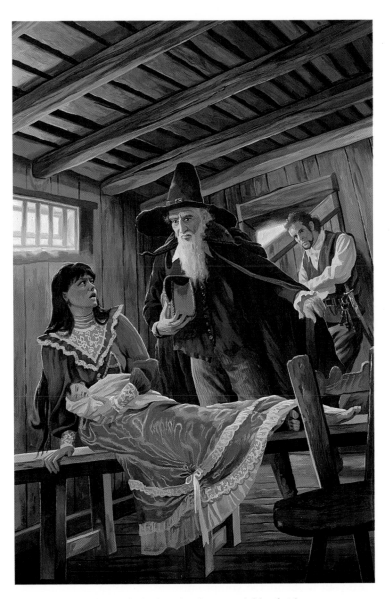

Hester looked at the doctor and felt afraid.

"I waited two years for you," Hester said. "Where were you?"

"I lived with the wild people in the woods and the mountains," the old man said. "I arrived in Boston this morning."

He looked quietly at the child on the bed, and Hester felt more afraid. "What are you going to do?" she asked him.

"I sent you here without me, and that was wrong," he answered. "I am a man of books—an old man—and I am ugly. Why did I marry you? You are young and beautiful . . ."

"I did not love you," Hester said. "You knew that."

"I know," the old man said. "But you were always in my heart. I loved you very much."

"I hurt you." Hester looked down at the floor. "I am sorry."

"No. I hurt you first," the doctor answered, "when I married you."

Hester was quiet. "I am not angry with you, Hester. You made a mistake. We all make mistakes. I understand. I only want to know one thing," Chillingworth said. "Who is the father of this child?"

Hester looked him in the eye and said, "Do not ask. You will never know."

"Will you never tell me?"

Hester looked away.

"Maybe the town will never know your secret," the old doctor said. "But I will find this man. I will know him when I see him. And then he will be mine!"

Hester saw a strange, ugly light in the old man's eyes. She put her hands over her heart.

"Do not be afraid," the old man said. "I will read the secret in the man's heart, not yours. I will not hurt him. I will not tell other people. But there is one thing, Hester. Everybody here thinks that I am Roger Chillingworth, a doctor. Tell nobody that I am your husband. Do you promise?"

"Why?" Hester asked. "Why not tell everybody? They will not punish you. I am the sinner, not you."

The old man had no answer to this. He only said, "Tell nobody my secret, and I will tell nobody yours."

"I promise," Hester said.

"Good. Now, I will leave you with your child and the scarlet letter."

With a strange smile on his tired old face, the doctor left the room.

Chapter 3   Little Pearl

A short time later, Hester left the prison. She moved into a small house outside the town. She had no friends, but she was always busy. She made beautiful clothes for her daughter. When people saw these clothes, they wanted Hester to make beautiful things for them, too. She started to get money from her work. She used some money for food, but she gave a lot of money away.

People said bad things to her when they saw her in the street. They were unfriendly when she visited their houses. Children followed her in town and shouted at her. Some people saw the scarlet letter on her breast and turned away. Church ministers looked coldly at her and talked to her about punishment and God. In their eyes, the scarlet letter shone red hot on her breast with fire from the Devil. Hester felt angry with the ministers, but she never showed her feelings. She always looked at the ground and walked away.

♦

Hester's daughter's name was Pearl. She was a wild and happy child. She often did not listen to her mother, but Hester never punished her. "I want her to be free," Hester thought. "As free as a bird in the sky."

Hester was sad because Pearl had no friends. But Pearl was

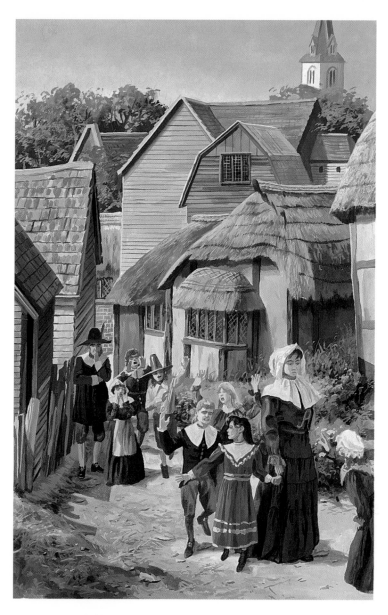

Children followed her in town and shouted at her.

strong. She held her mother's finger when she walked with her through town. She did not like other children. They were boring. They only played games about churches. Sometimes they shouted bad things at her mother. Pearl ran after them angrily and threw things at them. Then she came back happily and quietly to her mother.

One day, Pearl took some flowers. She threw one flower, then another flower, at the scarlet letter on her mother's breast. Hester looked sadly into little Pearl's wild eyes. After the last flower hit her mother's breast, Pearl laughed.

"Child, what are you?" Hester said.

"I am your little Pearl," the child answered.

"Are you really my child?"

The little girl laughed and danced up and down. "Yes. I am little Pearl."

"No," Hester said with a smile, "you are not really my little Pearl. Tell me, what are you? Who sent you to me?"

The child stopped dancing and looked up at her mother's face. "I do not know, Mother," she said. "*You* tell *me*."

"Your Father in Heaven sent you," Hester said.

Pearl put her finger on her mother's scarlet letter. "He did not send me," she said. "I have no Father in Heaven."

Then she laughed and started to dance again.

Chapter 4   The Governor's House

Some people in the town wanted to take Hester's daughter away. "Her mother is not teaching her the right things," they said.

Hester went with Pearl to a large house and met Governor Bellingham, the most important man in Boston. There were three other men with him: John Wilson, Arthur Dimmesdale, and Roger Chillingworth.

"You cannot take my daughter away!" Hester said.

"The girl has to live with another family," the Governor said. "She has to learn about God. You are a sinful woman. What can you do for the child?"

Hester put her hand on the scarlet letter. "I learn many things from this," she said. "I can teach my little Pearl."

"We have to take your child away *because* of that scarlet letter," the Governor said. "Don't you understand?"

"This letter teaches me important lessons every day," Hester said quietly. "The lessons will not help me because I am a sinner. But they will help my little child."

The Governor turned to John Wilson. "Mr. Wilson, what does the child know? Ask her some questions."

The old minister sat down in an armchair. He looked at Pearl in her little red dress and said, "Come here."

But Pearl ran to a window and stood there—a little red bird, ready to fly away.

"Pearl," the old minister said. "Can you tell me the answer to this question? Who made you?"

Pearl put her finger in her mouth and thought for a minute. Then she said, "Nobody made me. My mother found me in some wild flowers outside the prison door."

"Now do you understand?" Governor Bellingham turned angrily to Hester. "Your child knows nothing about God. You are teaching her nothing!"

But Hester took Pearl and held her. "God gave me the child!" she cried. "He took everything from me but He gave me little Pearl! Don't you understand? Pearl is my life. I love her and I will die without her. You will not take her!"

Then she turned to Arthur Dimmesdale, the young minister, and said, "You were my minister. You know me better than these men. I will not lose the child. Speak for me!"

Dimmesdale put his hand over his heart and turned to the Governor. "God gave her the child," he said. "The mother has to

Pearl ran to a window and stood there—a little red bird, ready to fly away.

show her child the way to Heaven. Then the child can bring her mother to Heaven, too. The sinful mother will be happier than the sinful father. Let us leave the mother with her child."

"You speak well, Mr. Dimmesdale," the Governor said. "The child will stay with her mother. But she has to learn about God. And when she is older, she will have to go to school."

Pearl then did a very strange thing. She left her mother and stood next to Arthur Dimmesdale. She took his hand and held it to her face. Hester looked at Pearl with the young minister and saw love in her daughter's heart. Suddenly, Pearl laughed and ran away. Hester followed her daughter out of the house.

"A strange child," said Roger Chillingworth. "You can easily see her mother in her. With a little careful study, I know that I can find the father, too."

"No, no," said John Wilson. "That is not right. God will find that secret, not us."

Chapter 5   Arthur Dimmesdale

The young minister, Arthur Dimmesdale, was a sick man. His face was always very white and his eyes were always tired. The townspeople were happy because Roger Chillingworth was his friend. "Maybe the old doctor can help him," they thought. Chillingworth moved into the same house as Dimmesdale. One day, Dimmesdale went into the doctor's room and sat at his window. The doctor worked at his desk and talked to the young minister. Suddenly, Dimmesdale heard a sound outside in the yard. He looked down and saw Pearl with her mother. The little girl ran and danced in the yard. She was as beautiful as the day.

Chillingworth left his desk and went to the window. "That girl threw water at the Governor yesterday," he said. "What is she, do you think? Does she come from God or from the Devil?"

The little girl ran and danced in the yard.

"I do not know," the young minister quietly said.

Suddenly, Pearl looked up and saw the two men at the window. She threw a flower up at them and laughed. Then she turned to her mother and said, "Come away, mother, or that old man will catch you! But he cannot catch little Pearl!"

Chillingworth walked away from the window and went back to his work. Then he said to the young minister, "I see you every day. You are sick, but in a very strange way. Sometimes I think that I know the answer. Sometimes I understand nothing about it. Can I ask you a question?"

"Of course."

"Do you have any secrets from me?"

"What do you mean?"

"Sometimes a man is sick because there are secrets in his heart," Chillingworth answered. Then he looked into the young minister's eyes and repeated, "Does *your* heart have any secrets, Mr. Dimmesdale?"

The young minister stood up angrily. "You are not a doctor of the heart!" he said.

"But how can I help you when you do not tell me everything?" the doctor said.

"I cannot tell you everything," the minister said. "Not you or anybody! Only God can help a man with a sick heart. You cannot stand between me and God!"

Without another word, he left the room.

Chillingworth smiled quietly. "This man's heart is full of fire," he thought. "There is something wild about him. I will study him carefully. I will find the secrets of his heart."

Later, Dimmesdale felt sorry. "Forgive me," he said to Chillingworth. "You wanted to help me, and I was angry with you. I was wrong. Please help me. I want to be well again."

"I will help you," the doctor said with a smile.

◆

One hot afternoon, Arthur Dimmesdale was asleep in a chair. Roger Chillingworth came into the room. He walked quietly across the floor and stood in front of the minister. He put his hand under the young man's shirt and did not move for a minute. Then he took his hand away and looked down at the minister with an icy smile. "I was right," he thought. "You have a secret in your heart. It is as hot as fire. But, dear Minister, it is not your secret now. It is mine, too! Your life is in my hands!"

Chapter 6   The Town Square at Night

Arthur Dimmesdale was a very sick man, but he was also the most famous minister in the town. His church was full every Sunday. "He is a wonderful speaker," people said. "He is a great man of God." Young women felt excited when he was near them. Old people were sad because he was weak and sick. "The minister will die before us," they said.

Every Sunday, Dimmesdale spoke to the people in church. He wanted to tell everybody the secret in his heart. He wanted people to hate him, but he was afraid. "I am a bad man," he told everybody. "I am the worst sinner in this town." But the people did not hate him. They loved him more and more. In their eyes, the young minister could do nothing wrong.

At home, the young man tried to kill the sick feeling in his heart. He did not eat or sleep for days. He was hungry, tired, and thirsty. He talked to God all night. Then, one night, he had an idea. He put on his best clothes and walked quietly out of the house.

Some time later, he arrived in the town square. He climbed up the stairs to the platform and looked out into the night. The town slept. Nobody could see him. "Hester Prynne stood here with a baby in her arms," he thought. "I will stand here now and wait for morning."

The minister stood there for an hour.

The minister stood there for an hour. He started to feel cold and weak. Suddenly he opened his mouth and shouted.

"That is better," he thought. "Now the town will wake up and find me on this platform. They will know the secret in my heart."

But nobody came. He saw a light at one of the windows in the Governor's house, but nothing more. Then, minutes later, he saw another light. This time it was in the street. It moved slowly into the square. Dimmesdale watched the light. "It is John Wilson," he thought. "He is in front of me but he cannot see me. Shall I talk to him?"

But the old minister walked past and Dimmesdale said nothing. "I shall wait here for the morning," he thought again. "Then people will see me and they will shout. They will jump from their beds. They will run into the square and look at me." The minister suddenly laughed when he thought about it. But then he heard a sound. It was another laugh, a child's laugh.

"Little Pearl?" he called. "Hester? Is that you?"

Suddenly, he saw Hester below him in the square. She stood below the platform and looked up at him. "Yes, it is me," she said.

"Where did you come from, Hester? What sent you here?"

"I was at Governor Winthrop's bed when he died. I make clothes for rich people when they die. It is my job," she said. "Now I am going home."

"Come up here, Hester," the minister said. "And you, little Pearl. You stood here seven years before, but I was not with you then. I want to be with you now."

Hester took her daughter's hand and climbed up next to the minister. Dimmesdale took Pearl's other hand. A strange feeling of new life came into his heart.

"Minister?" the little girl looked up and said.

"What is it, child?" Dimmesdale smiled down at her.

"Will you stand here with me and Mother tomorrow?"

"I cannot do that," the minister answered. "I will stand with you and your mother on another day, but not tomorrow."

Pearl tried to pull her hand away, but the minister's hand was strong. "Stay with me for one more minute," he said.

"Will you promise?" Pearl asked again. "Will you take my hand and mother's hand tomorrow?"

"Not tomorrow, Pearl. Another time."

"What other time?"

"One day, in front of God. But the daylight of this world cannot see your hand in mine."

At these words, Pearl gave a little laugh. At the same time, there was a sudden light in the sky. It shone down and lit the town in a strange, red light. Pearl laughed again. She took her hand away from the minister's.

"Look over there!" she said.

The minister followed the little girl's finger across the square. It was Roger Chillingworth. The light from the sky lit the old doctor's face. It was ugly with hate. The minister felt suddenly afraid.

"I hate that man, Hester," he said. "I really hate him. Who is he? Do you know him?"

Hester remembered her promise to her old husband and said nothing.

The red light in the sky started to die away.

"Who is he?" Dimmesdale repeated. "Can you do nothing for me? I am afraid of him. Help me, please."

"Minister," said little Pearl, "I know that man. I can tell you."

The minister put his ear down to Pearl's mouth, and listened. The little girl spoke into his ear, but it was not in English. It was another language, a baby's language. Then she laughed loudly.

"That is not funny, little Pearl," the minister said angrily.

"You did not promise," the small girl laughed. "You will not take my hand or mother's hand tomorrow!"

The light from the sky lit the old doctor's face. It was ugly with hate.

Before the minister could speak again, the old doctor called to him from across the square, "Mr. Dimmesdale, is that you?" He moved nearer to the platform and said, "We men of study have to be careful. We work too hard and walk in our sleep. Come, my dear friend, please. I will take you home."

"How did you find me here?" the minister asked, afraid. "Did you follow me?"

"I was on my way home from Governor Winthrop's house," Chillingworth answered. "I was with him when he died. I saw you here on this platform when that strange light shone in the sky. Now come with me, or you will feel very sick tomorrow. Then you will have to stay in bed, and you will not speak in church."

Without a word to Hester or to little Pearl, the young minister left the platform. He walked off into the night with Roger Chillingworth.

♦

The next day Arthur Dimmesdale spoke in church. He spoke beautifully. When he came out of the church, everybody wanted to talk to him. "Did you see the sky last night?" one man asked. "There was a letter of fire in the sky—a big, red letter 'A.' Did you see it?"

"No, I did not," the minister said. "I was asleep in bed."

Chapter 7   Punish or Forgive?

After that night in the town square, there was something new in Hester's life. She wanted to help Arthur Dimmesdale. "He is sicker than before," she thought. "He is getting weaker every day. He does not know that his friend, the old doctor, is really a very dangerous man. How can I help him? I cannot tell him that Chillingworth is my husband. But I have to do something."

One afternoon, Hester was with Pearl when she suddenly saw Chillingworth. "Go and play on the beach," Hester told Pearl. Then she went to the doctor and said, "I want to speak to you."

"Ah, Hester," Chillingworth smiled. "I hear many good things about you in the town. People say that you are a good, strong person with a warm heart. Yesterday, a friend of the old Governor—a good and intelligent man—spoke well of you. He thinks that maybe you can take the scarlet letter off your breast."

Hester studied the old man's face. Nine years earlier, he had a nice face. It was the face of an intelligent man with a love of books. But now his face was angry and unfriendly. It was the face of a hungry, wild animal. There was an ugly, red light in his eyes. He had the cold, thin smile of a man with ice in his heart.

"I do not want to talk about the scarlet letter," she said. "I want to talk about Arthur Dimmesdale."

"I am listening," Chillingworth said.

"For seven years I told nobody your name because I promised you. But you are doing bad things to Mr. Dimmesdale. You follow him everywhere. You are punishing him because you know the secret in his heart. You hold his life in your hands. He thinks that the Devil works in his heart. He thinks that God is punishing him. He does not know that it is you. I know now that my promise to you was a mistake."

"You cannot tell him my name," Chillingworth said with a dangerous smile. "Or I will tell the town his secret. Then they will put him in prison and kill him."

"That will be better than this. You are punishing him too much."

"That is not possible!" the old man said angrily. "I was a good man, happy with my books. Look at me now—a devil, yes! But who made me into this devil?"

"It was me," Hester said. "So why don't you punish me?"

Chillingworth put a long, thin finger on Hester's scarlet letter.

Chillingworth put a long, thin finger on Hester's scarlet letter. "You have this," he said.

Hester's face went red. She moved away from his hand and said, "I am going to tell Mr. Dimmesdale your secret."

"Be careful, Hester . . ." Chillingworth said.

But Hester held her head high and said, "You can tell the world about Mr. Dimmesdale and me. Maybe the world will forgive us one day. But you are a bad man with an ugly heart. You will never forgive. You will never stop punishing us."

Chillingworth looked at Hester quietly. For a minute she could almost see love in his eyes.

"I am sorry for you, Hester," he said with a warm, sad smile. "You are a good woman. I made a mistake when I married you. I was bad for you, I know."

"And I am sorry for you," Hester said sadly. "You were a good, intelligent man. I hurt you, and now you are a devil. Your heart is full of hate. I want nothing from you for me. But please—can't you be good again? Can't you forgive Mr. Dimmesdale for his sin? It will be good for your heart. It will make you a nice man again."

But Hester's warm words died in the ice of Chillingworth's heart. His face was ugly again, and the red light came back into his eyes. "Be quiet!" he shouted. "You brought the Devil into my life. I cannot take it away. God will forgive the two of you, but I will never forgive!"

With those words he turned from Hester and walked angrily away.

♦

"I hate him!" Hester thought, when the old man walked away. "He does worse things to me than I did to him."

She called Pearl from the beach.

"Why are you crying, Mother?" the little girl asked.

Hester sat down on the ground next to her daughter. She put

her finger on the scarlet letter and said, "What does this letter mean, Pearl? Do you know?"

"Of course I do, Mother. It is the great letter 'A.'"

"Why do I wear it? Can you tell me?"

"The minister holds his hand over his heart. You wear a scarlet letter over yours."

"Why do we do that? Do you know?"

"No." Pearl took her mother's hand and looked into her mother's eyes. "Will *you* tell *me*, Mother? Please?"

Hester looked at her daughter's pretty little face. "She is so wonderful," she thought. "I love her so much. I will not tell her that she was born in sin."

"Little Pearl," she smiled at her daughter. "These are strange questions. What do *I* know of the minister's heart? And why do I wear this scarlet letter? I wear it because it is beautiful."

But Pearl was not happy. She repeated the same question to her mother many times that day. And when she woke up in the morning, her first words to her mother were, "Why does the minister hold his hand over his heart?"

Chapter 8   In the Woods

Hester wanted to see Arthur Dimmesdale as quickly as possible. She wanted to tell him about Roger Chillingworth. But the minister was out of town. "He will be back tomorrow afternoon," somebody at the church told her.

So Hester took Pearl into the woods the next day, and waited for Arthur. She sat with Pearl under a large tree near a small river, and told her daughter a story. After a short time she heard a noise in the trees. "Go and play near the river," she told her daughter. "I want to speak to the minister."

The child ran to the river. Hester stood by a tree and waited for the minister. She was unhappy when she saw him. He walked

He walked very slowly, and his face was sad.

very slowly, and his face was sad. In town he usually tried to smile. But here, in the woods, his eyes were dead. They were without life, without hope.

"Arthur Dimmesdale," Hester called from behind the tree.

The minister stopped and looked around him. "Hester Prynne? Is that you?"

Hester walked to him and took his hand. It was as cold as ice. They walked hand in hand into the woods and sat under the large tree near the river.

"Hester," the minister said. "Are you happy?"

"Are *you*?" Hester answered.

"No. My life is without hope."

"The townspeople love you. You do good work. Doesn't that make you happy?"

"No. It only makes me more unhappy. People think that a light shines in my heart. But I know that my heart is as dark as night. I am a sinful man. The Devil laughs at me. My life is cold. I have to talk to somebody, but I have no friends."

"I am your friend," Hester said. "You can talk to me. But I have to tell you something important. You are living in the same house as a bad and dangerous man."

"What do you mean?"

"Oh, Arthur, forgive me. I have a secret from you. I could not tell you before today because I made a promise. But I was wrong and I am sorry." Hester took his hand and put it over the scarlet letter on her breast. "Arthur, I have to tell you. It is about the old man—the doctor. You think that he is Roger Chillingworth. But that is not his name. His name is Prynne. He is my husband!"

The minister took his hand away from Hester's. He looked at her with dark, angry eyes. "How could you do this to me?" he said. "I live with that man. He sees into my heart. He is your husband and you did not tell me. I cannot forgive you for this!"

Hester threw her arms around Arthur and held his head to her breast. He tried to move away, but Hester did not want to lose him. "You will forgive me!" she cried. "The world hates me. God hates me. I can live with that. But you cannot hate me, too, Arthur. I cannot live with that."

Hester held him for some minutes. Then Arthur looked up into her face. He was not angry with her now. "I forgive you, Hester," he said sadly. "God knows that we are not the worst people in the world. Roger Chillingworth is worse than us. That man's heart is blacker than our sin. You and I, Hester, we never wanted to hurt anybody."

"Never," Hester said. "Our sin was born in love, not hate. Do you remember?"

"I remember."

They sat quietly for a long time in the dark green light. There was only the sound of the river, and the wind in the treetops high above their heads.

Suddenly, Arthur turned to Hester. "Roger Chillingworth knows that you will tell me his secret. What will he do now, do you think? Will he tell the townspeople that I am the father of your child?"

"I think that he will try to hurt us in another way," said Hester.

"I hate him," Arthur said. "The Devil sent him to us. Oh Hester, you are strong. Think for me. What can I do?"

"You have to go away," she said. "Leave the town. Be free. A ship brought you here from England. A ship can take you back."

Arthur thought about this for a minute, and then he said, "I am weak and sick. I cannot go. It is too late for me."

"I will go with you," Hester quietly said.

Arthur looked into her eyes, and suddenly his heart was happy. "Oh, Hester," he said. "Now this will be a better life for us. Why didn't we think of it before?"

"Do not think about yesterday," Hester said. "Let's begin a new life now!" She took the scarlet letter from her breast and threw it into the trees. Then she took off her white hat. Her thick, dark hair fell around her face.

"And now," she said, "you have to know our little Pearl. You will see her now with new eyes."

"Will she want to know me?"

"She will love you," Hester answered. She turned away and called Pearl's name. Pearl came out of the woods and stood across the river. She looked quietly at her mother and the minister.

"Come, dear child," her mother said. "Here is my friend. He will be your friend, too. Jump across the river. Come to us."

But Pearl did not move. She looked across the water. She did not take her eyes off her mother's dress.

"Strange child," Hester said. "Why don't you come?"

Again, no answer.

"Be quick, or I will be angry with you."

Pearl suddenly fell to the ground and started to cry. Hester understood. She looked sadly at Pearl and said, "Look down at your feet—there in front of you."

Pearl stopped her noise. She stood up and saw the scarlet letter on the ground.

"Bring it here," her mother called.

"No," her daughter answered angrily. "You come here and get it."

Hester walked to the river. She took the scarlet letter from the ground and put it back on her breast. "Is that better?" she smiled sadly at her daughter. "Your mother is sad again. Will you come to her now?"

"Yes. Now I will," the child answered. She jumped across the small river and held her mother in her arms. "Now you are my mother again," she said. "And I am your little Pearl."

Hester held Pearl by the hand and took her to the minister. "Will you go back with us into the town?" the little girl asked him.

"Strange child," Hester said. "Why don't you come?"

Arthur kissed her little face and said, "Not now, dear child." Pearl looked at him angrily for a minute. Then she ran away and washed her face in the river.

Chapter 9   Music in the Square

The minister went back to town. He went to an office near the ocean and he asked about ships to England. "There is one ship," the man in the office told him. "It is going to England in four days."

"That is good," Dimmesdale thought. "There is a big party for the new Governor in three days. Everybody has a day's vacation, and I have to speak in church. After that, I can go away on the ship with Hester and Pearl."

At home, Roger Chillingworth came into Dimmesdale's room. "Your face is tired," he said. "Can I give you something? You have to be strong when you speak in church."

"I do not want your help, thank you," Arthur told him. "I feel better."

The doctor did not understand, but he said, "I am happy. My help was good for you."

"Yes. You are a good friend. Thank you for everything," the minister said. "But now I have to work. I have to speak in church in three days. It is an important day and I have to write my notes."

Chillingworth left the room. The minister took some papers from his desk and threw them onto the fire. "I want to say something different," he thought. "I will write something better than that." He sat down and started to write. His pen danced across the pages through the night.

♦

Three days later, Hester and Pearl went into town. The town square was full of people.

"Why are these people here?" Pearl asked her mother.

"Everybody has a day's vacation," Hester said. "The new Governor will go past in a minute. You will see the important people of Boston. There will be a lot of music."

"Will I see the minister, too?" Pearl asked. "Will he hold my hand?"

"He will be here, but he will not hold your hand today."

"He is a strange, sad man," Pearl said. "He holds my hand in the middle of the night. He kisses me in the woods. But on a sunny day in the center of town, he does not want to know me."

"Be quiet, Pearl," Hester said. "You do not understand these things. But do not think about the minister now. Look at everybody. Look at their happy faces!"

Suddenly, a man stood next to Hester. His face was brown from the sun and he wore dirty, old clothes.

"One more person is coming on my ship with us to England," he said.

Hester turned her head. The man smiled at her, and his mouth was full of black teeth. "What do you mean?" she said.

"I spoke to Doctor Chillingworth. He is coming with us, too. He tells me that he is a good friend of the minister. I am happy. Another doctor on my ship will be useful."

The man from the ship walked away, and Hester suddenly felt sick and weak. She closed her eyes. When she opened them again, she saw Roger Chillingworth. He stood across the square. He smiled at her through the noisy crowd. It was an ugly smile, full of secret meaning.

♦

Suddenly, above the noise of the crowd, Hester heard the sound of music. Everybody shouted happily when the important people in the town walked into the square. Pearl was very excited and

He looked at Hester and Pearl and the crowd was very quiet.

danced to the music. Then Hester saw Arthur Dimmesdale. For the first time in many years, his hand was not over his heart. He held his head high, and there was color in his face.

Arthur and the other important people went into the church. Hester waited in the square next to the high platform. An hour later, people started to leave the church. Everybody was excited.

"The minister spoke beautifully," said one person.

"He was wonderful," another person said.

The music started again and the important people walked slowly away from the church.

When the minister came out of the church, Hester put her hand to her mouth.

"Oh, no!" she thought. "What happened?"

Other people in the crowd looked at the minister, too. His face was suddenly very white. His eyes were dark and he moved very slowly. John Wilson, the old minister, said, "Be careful, Mr. Dimmesdale. You are going to fall." He took his arm, but Arthur pushed him away.

Then he slowly turned and walked weakly into the crowd. Minutes later he stopped in front of the platform. He looked at Hester and Pearl and the crowd was very quiet.

"What is he doing?" they wanted to know. "Why is he looking at the woman and her child so strangely?"

Suddenly, Arthur held his hands out to Hester. "Hester," he said. "Come here. Come here, my little Pearl."

Pearl flew into his arms as quickly as a little bird. Hester walked more slowly. At that minute, Roger Chillingworth pushed through the crowd and took the minister's arm.

"What are you doing?" he said angrily in the minister's ear. "Are you crazy? Push that woman away!"

But the minister turned to the old doctor and said, "You are too late. I am not yours now. With God's help, I will be free of

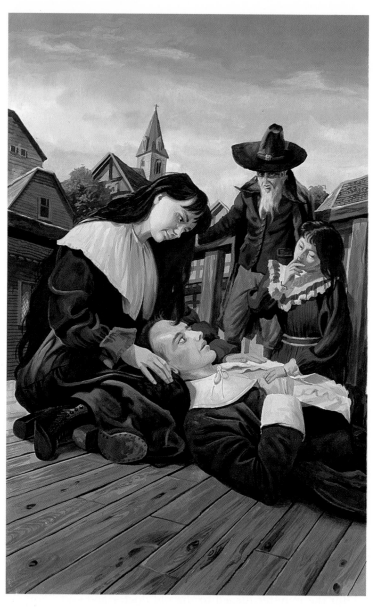

"Will you kiss your father now?"

you." He then turned back to Hester and said, "Hester Prynne, in the name of God, come with me now. Help me onto this platform."

The young minister put one hand on Hester's arm. He took little Pearl's hand in his other hand. The three of them walked up the stairs to the platform. The crowd was very interested. Some people were angry. Most people said nothing.

On the platform, Arthur turned to Hester and said, "Isn't this better than our trip to England?"

"Better?" Hester said. "We will die now, and little Pearl will die with us. Is that really better?"

"Hester, I am dying," the minister said. "When I die, I will take our sin with me."

Then he turned to the crowd in the square and said loudly, "People of New England. You loved me, but look at me now— the one sinner of the world. I did not stand here before, and I was wrong."

After he spoke, he did a very strange thing. With a small smile, he opened his shirt to the crowd. People pushed excitedly nearer the platform. They all wanted to see the minister. Arthur stood there with his shirt open. Then he fell. Hester went down next to him. Roger Chillingworth jumped up onto the platform. He went down to the floor and said into the minister's ear, "You got away from me."

"God forgive you," Arthur said. "You are a sinner, too. The biggest sinner of us all."

Then he turned his eyes away from the old man and looked up at his daughter's face.

"Don't be sad, my little Pearl," he said weakly. "Will you kiss your father now?"

Pearl moved her face down to her father's face and kissed him on the mouth.

Hester kissed him, too, then quietly said, "You can see Heaven now. Tell me, what can you see? Shall we never meet again?"

"I do not know, dearest Hester," he said. "We sinned. We forgot our God. I am afraid. I am very afraid . . ."

And with those words, the minister closed his eyes and died.

Chapter 10   Only Love

After Arthur died, Hester and Pearl left Boston. Roger Chillingworth died two or three months later. He left a lot of money to Pearl.

People talked for many years about that day in the town square. Each person told a different story.

"God put a scarlet letter 'A' on the minister's breast," said some people.

"Roger Chillingworth put it there," other people said.

Many people said, "I saw nothing."

One afternoon, many years later, some children played outside Hester's old house. Suddenly, they saw an old woman. She wore a long, gray dress with a scarlet letter on her breast. She walked slowly past them and went inside the house.

Hester Prynne was in Boston again. But where was little Pearl? Nobody knew. But letters came for Hester from another country. One day, Hester started to make white clothes for a baby.

For many years she lived in her small house outside town. She made clothes and gave them away. She helped many unhappy women with their problems.

"One day," she told them, "when God is ready, there will be a new world—a better world for women. We will be the same as men. Everybody will understand that only love can make us happy. One day. But not today."

ACTIVITIES

Chapters 1–2

Before you read

1 Read the Introduction and answer these questions.
   a What is the "scarlet letter"?
   b Who is the father of Hester's child?
   c Why do you think Hester is afraid of an old man?
2 Was life very different for women in the 1600s, do you think? Was it better or worse than today? How?
3 Look at the Word List at the back of the book. Find new words in your dictionary.
   a Which are words for a person?
   b Which is a word for a lot of people?

While you read

4 Are these sentences right (✓) or wrong (✗)?
   a The prison is in the town center.   .....
   b The people of Boston hate Hester.   .....
   c Hester was born in New England.   .....
   d Hester came to Boston without her husband.   .....
   e Hester knows the name of her child's father.   .....
   f People know that Chillingworth is Hester's husband.   .....

After you read

5 Why:
   a is Hester in prison?
   b is she going to stand in the town square?
   What:
   c do the ministers want Hester to do?
   d does Hester promise Chillingworth?
   Who:
   e is Arthur Dimmesdale?
   f is the old man in the crowd?
   Where:
   g does Chillingworth visit Hester?
   h did he live for two years?

6 Work with another student. Look at the pictures in Chapters 1 and 2. What can you see in each picture?

7 Discuss these questions. What do you think? Why:

    a are the people of Boston angry with Hester? Are they right?

    b doesn't Hester tell them the name of her child's father?

    c does Chillingworth have a "strange, ugly light in his eyes"?

Chapters 3–4

Before you read

8 Discuss this question. What problems will Hester have when she leaves prison?

While you read

9 Which is the right word?

    a Hester doesn't have any *friends/ money*.

    b Hester sells *clothes/ flowers* to the townspeople.

    c Pearl is a *happy/ sad* child.

    d The Governor thinks that Hester is a *good/ bad* mother.

    e *Chillingworth/ Dimmesdale* wants the child to stay with Hester.

    f John Wilson *wants/ does not want* Chillingworth to find the child's father.

After you read

10 Finish these sentences. Put the words in the right place. Who is speaking or thinking? Who or what are they thinking about?

    a "I want her to be *sky/ free/ a/ the/ bird/ as/ as/ in*."

    b "Her mother *the/ things/ not/ her/ right/ is/ teaching*."

    c "This letter *things/ every/ me/ teaches/ day/ important*."

    d "My mother found me *outside/ the/ in/ prison/ flowers/ wild/ some/ door*."

    e "The mother has to *Heaven/ the/ to/ her/ show/ child/ way*."

11 Work with another student. Have this conversation between the Governor and Hester.

    Student A: You are the Governor. You want Hester and Pearl to leave Boston. Tell Hester why.

    Student B: You are Hester. You do not want to leave Boston. Tell the Governor why.

Chapters 5–6

Before you read

12 Look at the pictures in these chapters. Who is the child's father, do you think? Will Chillingworth find him? How will he try?

While you read

13 What happens first? Number these sentences, 1–8.

    a Dimmesdale stops eating and sleeping.   .....

    b Dimmesdale watches Hester and Pearl in the yard.   .....

    c Dimmesdale goes to the town square at night.   .....

    d Chillingworth moves into Dimmesdale's house.   .....

    e Hester and Pearl stand next to Dimmesdale.   .....

    f There is a strange light in the town.   .....

After you read

14 Who or what are these sentences about?

    a Chillingworth is his new friend.

    b Pearl laughs at them.

    c It is as hot as fire.

    d He wants people to hate him.

    e Her hand gives new life to Dimmesdale's heart.

    f His face is ugly with hate.

    g The townspeople see it in the sky.

15 Work with another student. Have this conversation between Chillingworth and Dimmesdale.

    Student A: You are Chillingworth. Ask Dimmesdale about his night in the town square with Hester and Pearl. You know his secret, but you want him to tell you.

    Student B: You are Dimmesdale. Answer Chillingworth's questions, but don't tell him your secret.

Chapters 7–8

Before you read

16 How does Hester feel after the night in the town square? What will she do now, do you think? Why? Write notes about three possible plans.

While you read

17 Are these sentences about Chillingworth (C) or Dimmesdale (D)?

    a Hester wants to help him. .....
    b Hester meets him on a beach. .....
    c He thinks that God is punishing him. .....
    d Hester wants him to forgive. .....
    e Hester meets him in the woods. .....
    f Hester tells him a secret. .....

After you read

18 Finish these sentences.

    a The townspeople are beginning to like Hester because ...
    b Hester hates her husband because ...
    c Chillingworth is angry with Dimmesdale because ...
    d Dimmesdale is angry with Hester because ...
    e Dimmesdale hates Chillingworth because ...
    f Dimmesdale suddenly feels happy because ...
    g Pearl is angry with her mother because ...
    h Pearl washes her face in the river because ...

19 Put these words in the right sentences.

beautiful   dangerous   hungry   nice   sad   sinful   strong   warm

a The townspeople say that Hester has a .... heart.

b Nine years ago, Chillingworth had a .... face.

c Now Chillingworth has the face of a .... animal.

d Hester thinks that her husband is a .... man.

e Hester tells Pearl that the scarlet letter is ....

f Dimmesdale thinks that he is a .... man.

g Dimmesdale thinks that Hester is ....

h Pearl is happy when her mother is ....

Chapters 9–10

Before you read

20 Will the story end sadly or happily, do you think? Work with two other students and tell the story.

While you read

21 Put one word in each sentence.

a Dimmesdale finds a ship to ....

b He is going to leave with Hester and ....

c .... is going on the ship, too.

d Dimmesdale speaks .... in church.

e Then he goes up the stairs to the .... in the square.

f He opens his .... to the crowd.

g Pearl .... her father.

h Dimmesdale closes his eyes and ....

After you read

22 Discuss these questions with another student.

a Is Dimmesdale a strong man? Why (not)?

b Does Chillingworth want the townspeople to know the name of Pearl's father? Why (not)?

c Dimmesdale says that Chillingworth is "the biggest sinner of us all." Why does he say that? Is he right?

d Hester says that "only love can make us happy." What does she mean? Is she right?

Writing

23 You are Roger Chillingworth. Write about your first day in Boston.

24 You are Dimmesdale. Your new friend, Chillingworth, is moving into your house (Chapter 5). Write a letter to a friend about him.

25 You work for a Boston newspaper. After Dimmesdale dies, write about his life for your newspaper.

26 What mistakes do Dimmesdale, Chillingworth, and Hester make in the story? Write about them. Who makes the worst mistakes?

27 What do Hester and Pearl do in the years after Dimmesdale dies? Write the story.

28 You are Pearl at the end of the story. Write a letter to your mother in Boston. What do you remember about your early years in Boston? Tell her.

29 You are Hester at the end of the story. Pearl invites you to live with her in another country. You don't want to leave Boston. Why not? Write Pearl a letter.

30 Hester says, "One day there will be a new world—a better world for women." Is the world a good place for women today, do you think? Why (not)? Write about this for a student magazine.

WORD LIST *with example sentences*

adulteress (n) She is an *adulteress* and she isn't going to marry her lover.

breast (n) She carried the baby at her *breast*.

crowd (n) I can't move in this *crowd*!

devil (n) He is a very bad man. People say that he does the *Devil's* work!

forgive (v) He said sorry, but I couldn't *forgive* him.

god (n) Some people go to church when they want to talk to *God*.

governor (n) George Bush was the *governor* of Texas.

heart (n) He has to walk very slowly because he has a weak *heart*.

heaven (n) Will I go to *Heaven* after I die?

hold (v) My daughter is afraid. Please *hold* her hand.

kiss (v) He *kissed* his children and said goodbye.

minister (n) We talked with the *minister* when we left the church.

pearl (n) She only wears her *pearls* when she goes to the theater.

platform (n) He climbed up onto the *platform* and began to speak.

prison (n) He killed a man and went to *prison*.

promise (n/v) There will be no parties in this house when we are on vacation. Give me your *promise*!

punish (v) Our teacher *punished* us when our homework was late.

scarlet (adj) She wore a black dress and a beautiful *scarlet* coat.

secret (n) I can't tell you about my mother's problem. It's a *secret*.

sin (n) He went to church and told people about his *sins*. He is a *sinful* man, but now people understand.